This is me...

(draw or stick a picture of yourself in the cloud)

My name is...

My age is...

My address is...

(fill in the white stripes on the shooting stars)

This book is dedicated to
Ike, Lily, Poppy and Jacob,
our little inspirations!

I Feel Good About Me!

All rights reserved. No part of this publication may be reproduced or transmitted by any means, electronic, mechanical, photocopying or otherwise without the prior permission of the publisher.
Printed in Great Britain by Safair Print Services, Woolwich, London SE18 6RS.
Published in 2007 by Feel Good Friends, Greenwich, London.
© Amy Rogers 2006 • Illustrations © Lucy Rogers 2007 • Design by proudspark.co.uk
A CIP record for this book is available from the British Library.
ISBN 978-0-9556426-1-6

My house looks like this...

These are the people I live with...

(draw pictures or stick photographs in the frames)

My school is called...

My teacher is called...

At school my favourite things are...

Feel Good Primary

At playtime I play...

My best friends are...

(draw a picture of your friends in the space above)

My favourite songs are...

My favourite flowers are...

My favourite toys are...

These are the games I like playing...

These are my pets...

If I could have any pet in the world it would be...

(fill in the circles with words or pictures)

If I had three wishes they would be...

1

2

3

(write your wishes in the stars)

If I could meet a famous person it would be...

If I was magic I would...

I would like to dress up as...

This is the house I would most like to live in...

(draw your dream house below)

When I grow up I would like to be...

If I could drive I would like a car like this...
(park your dream car next to Roly's)

These are the things
that make me happy...

These are the things
I enjoy doing...

I am lucky
because...

(fill in the clouds)

These are the things that make me sad...

These are the things that make me laugh...

These are the things I am good at...

My favourite colours are...

My favourite books are...

My favourite animals are...

My favourite films are...

(fill in the flags with words or pictures)

These are three of my favourite memories...

1

2

3

(write down your memories in the stars)

These are the foods I like...

Yummy Menu

These are the foods I don't like...

Yucky Menu

When I was a baby I looked like this...

When I am a grown up I think I will look like this...

(draw or stick a picture in the frames above)

These are all the people that care about me...

These are the kind things that people have done for me...

These are the kind things that I have done for other people...

(fill in the hearts)

These are the things that I do to make my friends laugh...

These are the things that I do to cheer my friends up if they are sad...

These are all the things
that I am proud of...

(fill in the clouds)

These are the things that
make me feel calm...

My favourite
place to go is...

I look after my world by...

I think the world would be a better place if...

These are all the countries I would like to visit...

(fill in the stars)

I am amazing because...

I am important because...

I am loving because...

I look after my body by...

Things that make me excited are...

(fill in the circles)

Photographs or drawings of me Feeling Good!!!

(draw or stick photographs in the frames)

These are all the things I would like to do in the future...

1. ....
2. ....
3. ....
4. ....
5. ....
6. ....
7. ....
8. ....
9. ....
10. ....

The future is so bright I need shades!!

(draw a picture of yourself around the glasses)

The rest of the fabulous Feel Good Friends product range...

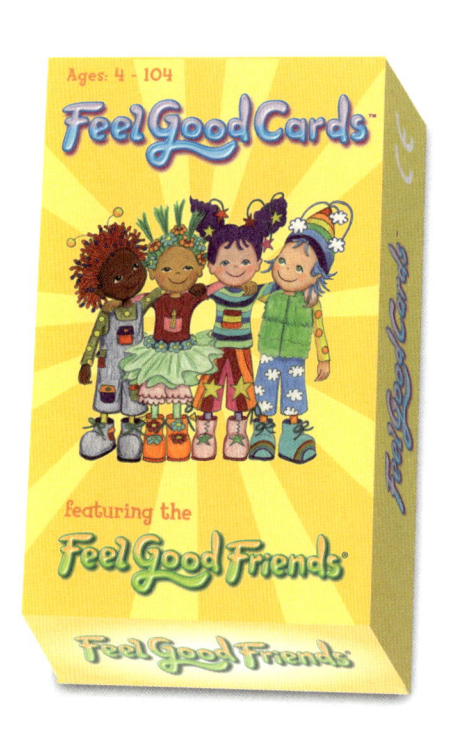

FEEL GOOD FACES BOARD GAME

This is a non competitive team game helping children to become familiar with different feelings and emotions and ways of expressing them.
A fun way for children to gain confidence and self esteem. Children will be sharing, caring, laughing and smiling whilst focusing on their own and others unique qualities.

FEEL GOOD CARDS

Saying regular affirmations can change your thinking pattern from negative to positive. This will help children to Feel Good about themselves making them happier and better able to cope with any problems they might face. The cards can be used in many different ways; such as choosing one at bedtime to enable sleeping on a positive thought, first thing in the morning to start the day positively or stuck around the bedroom or classroom walls!

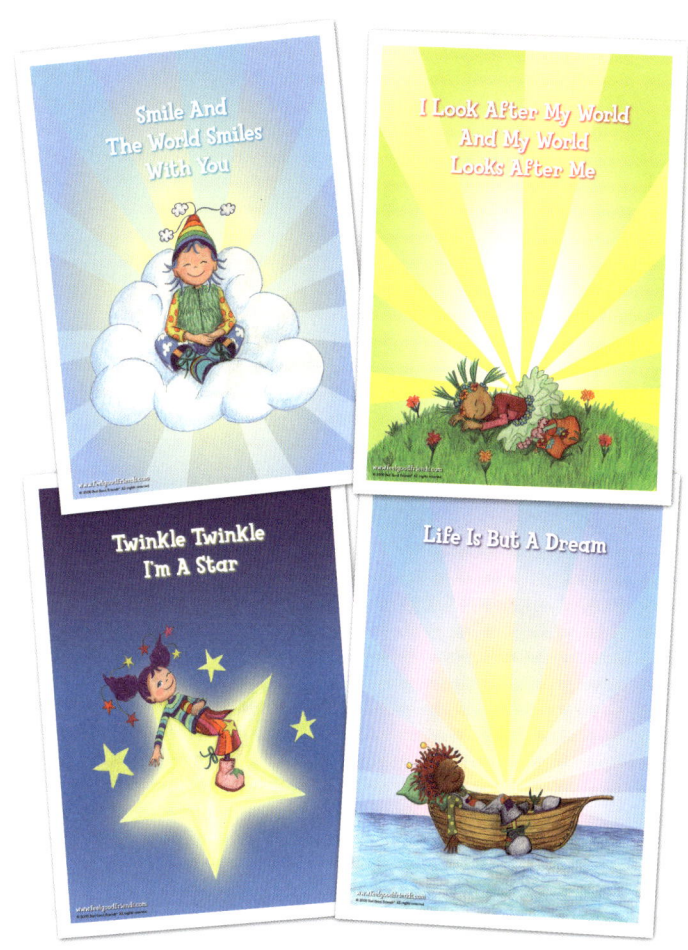

FEEL GOOD JOURNEYS

A relaxation CD with four separate magical journeys which each benefit children in a different way.

They can fly through the night with Betty Brightstar, go on a desert Island adventure with Pippin Pocket, dance around the garden with Tiggy Tutu and float on a cloud with Roly Rainbow. The CD uses a combination of creative visualisation, breathing techniques, colour therapy and affirmations to instill positive beliefs and release tension in the body and mind.

FEEL GOOD POSTERS

Bright, colourful A3 posters of the Feel Good Friends with a simple positive affirmation. A great way to decorate the bedroom or classroom and send out Feel Good messages.

All enquiries...

020 8854 7767

Prices and online ordering at...

www.feelgoodfriends.com